COMPUTER TECHNOLOGY FOR HIGHER EDUCATION

VOLUME ONE
An Overview

COMPUTER TECHNOLOGY FOR HIGHER EDUCATION

Volume One	:	**An Overview**
Volume Two	:	**The Indian Experience**
Volume Three	:	**The Canadian Experience**

COMPUTER TECHNOLOGY FOR HIGHER EDUCATION

A Design Model for a Computerizing University

Volume I
An Overview

Sarla Achuthan
Binod C. Agrawal
Vimal P. Shah
R.P. Soni
S.R. Thakore

W. David Chandler
Barbara Kaltz
Murray Knuttila
R. Brien Maguire
William A. Stahl
Larry R. Symes

Concept Publishing Company, New Delhi 110059 (India)

ISBN-81-7022-466-7 (Set)
ISBN 81-7022-467-5 (Vol. I)

First Published 1993

Published and Printed by
Ashok Kumar Mittal
Concept Publishing Company
A/15-16, Commercial Block, Mohan Garden
NEW DELHI-110059 (India)
Phones: 5554042, 5504042

PREFACE

The effects of computerization on society have continually been underestimated, as has been the pace of innovation. This project has attempted to look at how computerization affects universities and the society that they serve from the perspective of two countries situated on opposite sides of the globe. The goal was to improve the effective utilization of technology within the university systems in both Canada and India.

It is hoped that the results of the project will be of use to all members of the university community and to all government planners involved with education throughout the world as they establish the role technology will assume in the universities of the $21^{st.}$ century.

The effort required to establish and accomplish a joint collaborative project such as this should not be underestimated. Almost five years were required to put the project together, and another five years were devoted to its execution. During that time the assistance and encouragement of a large number of individuals were required. To each of them we are deeply indebted and wish to express our thanks.

As this has been a joint venture between two national groups, the lives of the participants have been enriched in ways that were not anticipated. For this we are all thankful.

R. P. Soni,
Project Director, India

L. R. Symes,
Project Director, Canada

October 1992

Table of Contents

Introduction

This project focuses on the complex task of computerizing universities. Over the past eight years the Indian and Canadian teams have worked towards two goals. The first, this three-volume document, is a design model for use as a planning and implementation tool for the university computerization process. The term "model" is not used here in the mathematical sense, nor does it present any fixed pattern of organization considered necessary for computerizing a university. Rather, it examines various aspects of computerization, lays down assumptions underlying the broad objectives of computerization, indicates crucial issues to be examined, and explores the possible pathways decision-makers may follow. The model has been jointly developed, building upon both the Canadian and Indian experience of computerization in higher education. Its aim is to enable university decision-makers to comprehend the process and changes involved in university computerization. As a result, the model addresses the technical, organizational and social dimensions of the process. The second goal was to increase the cadre of trained university and computer personnel. This was achieved through a series of training programmes held at the University of Regina in May and June of 1990, 1991, and 1992 as well as the establishment in 1991, with the assistance of the Digital Equipment Corporation of India, of the Computer Training and Applications Laboratory (COMTAL) at the University of Gujarat, Ahmedabad, and the support of its ongoing training programmes.

The inception of this project occurred at a Regina board meeting of the Shastri Indo-Canadian Institute in the spring of 1984. The Indian High Commissioner to Canada, Mr. Fabian, Dr. Alex Guy, Deputy Minister of the Saskatchewan Government Department of Science and Technology, and Dr. Roland Miller of Luther College, University of Regina proposed a collaborative project to study computerization in higher education. With a startup grant from the Government of Saskatchewan, four members of the University of Regina travelled to Montreal in June 1985 to attend a Shastri Institute sponsored conference, where they met with Dr. Gunvant Shah of South Gujarat University, Surat and through him contacted Dr. Madhuri Shah, chair of the University Grants Commission (UGC) of India, who sanctioned an international seminar to be held at South Gujarat University, Surat, in February 1987. Subsequently the International Development Research Council funded the Canadian team's further development of a collaborative project and its participation in the seminar. Discussions initiated at Surat culminated in a meeting at Gujarat University in Ahmedabad in June 1988 at which it was agreed that the Canadian and Indian teams should submit proposals to the Canadian International Development Agency (CIDA) and UGC, respectively.

The proposals were submitted in July (India) and October (Canada) 1988. Approval for three-year projects came from CIDA in March 1989 and from UGC in November 1989. In August 1989 the first full meeting of the two research teams was held in Regina to operationalize the training and research activities.

Several methodologies were used in developing the design model. Surveys were conducted in Canada and India to establish a baseline for computerization in both countries. The Indian team followed up its survey with 18 case studies of technical and research institutions and universities. Both teams conducted pedagogical experiments, and incorporated the experience of the training programmes. A substantial body of literature on computerization was compiled and analyzed. The two teams conducted their research in parallel, sharing their findings periodically by mail, electronically and at joint team meetings held in Ahmedabad in August 1990 and in Regina in August 1992.

The design model is presented in three parts. This volume is an overview and synthesis, which brings together our joint recommendations for the process of computerization. It is the result of an intense collaborative effort reflecting a consensus of the two teams. The second and third volumes present more detailed analyses of the research upon which these recommendations are based. The second volume examines the Indian experience of computerization; the third does the same for Canada.

The Social Context of Computerization

The process of computerizing a single university or an entire system of higher education involves changes in both technology and human social relations. Computerization, as the term is used here, is a process of acquisition, use and application of computers in the university or another institution of higher learning for efficient and effective teaching, research and administration. Careful planning is required because there are many misconceptions and misunderstandings, as well as unrealistic expectations, as to what computers can do.

When considering the process of computerization, it is essential to understand that the university is a unique institution with its own history, traditions, structures and modes of operation, while at the same time part of a larger historical, cultural, social, economic and political setting. The educational system, and the use of computers, will continue to influence each other. It is important, therefore, that all participants in the decision-making process have a basic grasp of the socioeconomic, political, and historical contexts of the university.

The decision to computerize or not raises a number of crucial issues. Though not all of these are dealt with in detail in this study, decision-makers in a society desiring computerization of its higher education system must pay attention to what is feasible, given the present day developments in information technology, and their socioeconomic industrial context, including the current level of computerization. In addition, recognizing that there often are gender, class, caste, racial and regional differences and inequalities within society, attention will have to be given to concerns about whether computerization results in reducing these differences and inequalities or increasing them. It is also important to ask what individual and societal benefits will accrue from computerization. Finally, the nature and extent of the computer competence of entering students will have to be considered since the process of computerization of the higher education system builds on this existing knowledge.

As the process of computerization proceeds, many decisions will have to be made, decisions which will raise key issues concerning the very nature of the university. Among them:

1. What is the social role of higher education? What are its priorities and objectives?

2. Who sets the goals and priorities for higher education?

3. What share of a society's resources should be devoted to higher education?

4. How should decision-making in higher education be structured?

5. Whom does and should the higher education system serve?

6. What are the possibilities for resistance and adaptation to the changes brought about by computerization?

7. What are the relative roles of the university and the private sector in meeting the computer educational needs of society?

These and other key questions can be answered from a number of different perspectives making it necessary to understand that many of the debates that emerge throughout the process of computerization are, in reality, reflections of the differing theoretical perspectives which people hold regarding the organization of the university and society as a whole.

The reports, analyses and recommendations which follow draw on the experiences of societies that have begun and are "well on their way" in the process of computerizing their higher education systems. As was noted, not all of the larger social contextual issues are explicitly dealt with in what follows. Nevertheless, these issues are considered important and they represent a backdrop for much of the material and the discussions presented here. We have assumed that the decision to computerize has been made. Our question is how to make computerization effective. We assume a situation of managed (or at least semi-managed) change. That is, we presume that the university will follow a plan in its process of computerization. Today's situation is complex and careful planning is necessary to avoid inefficiency and the waste of scarce resources. The purpose of this part of the design model is to highlight the process of change involved in university computerization.

The Process of Computerization

To help achieve the greatest benefit in the computerization process, we conclude the following:

1. There are several ways of speaking about computerization. One which is particularly useful speaks of the process of computerization as building a network* University decision-makers must weave together various

*Not to be confused with LAN's, Ethernet, Bitnet or other forms of linking machines discussed elsewhere.

technical components with people's needs and interests, incorporating both into the plan for computerization.

2. There is no simple formula or one "right way" to go about computerization. It is a long process of consultation and negotiation, made particularly difficult, on the one hand, by the unpredictability and rapid change in the elements (both technical and human) which make up the network, and, on the other hand, by inertia and resistance to change within the organization. Balance and judgement are required.

3. In order to enlist people into the network, decision-makers must first ask three questions: What are people's attitudes toward computers within the institution? Are there product champions who can be mobilized for support? What value commitments are involved? As pointed out later, enroling product champions is crucial to the success of the computerization plan.

4. An effective process of computerization requires that user needs be addressed. User values should not simply replace virtuosity or economic ones (see Volume III, *The Canadian Experience*). Rather, university decision-makers must pay attention to all three value sets in building the computerization network. Doing so necessitates the participation of users in decisions regarding computerization. Value conflicts are likely to be particularly difficult to deal with.

5. The problem of resource allocation is not one of simple cost benefit analysis in the strict economic sense, but one of finding the most effective way to build the computerization network. Four elements will form the building blocks of the network—3people, technology, money, and space. The most crucial element is people. The success or failure of university computerization depends upon the quality of the people who make and execute the plan.

6. The significance of training cannot be over-emphasized. Unless computer users have been adequately trained they will be inefficient, unhappy and their full potential will not be realized. Training needs to be more than formal instruction; informal training and consultation involving product champions and other co-workers are essential.

Computers in Teaching

Computer technology has considerable potential to enhance university teaching and to provide a better learning environment, in particular when the unique capabilities of this technology are adequately exploited. The recommendations with respect to the use of computers for teaching are based on the following findings and assumptions:

1. Teaching and research are closely related activities within the academic function of the university.

2. Computer use related to teaching in universities includes teaching of students and training of faculty.

3. Computing in teaching includes both teaching **about** computers (such as in Computer Science, Engineering or Business Administration programmes) and teaching **with** computers (instructional computing, i.e. using computers to aid in teaching the subject matter of any discipline). These teaching activities may occur at a variety of levels, leading to various degrees of computer competence. Computers may be used for teaching in any discipline (including Computer Science) both on-campus and off-campus (distance education), in the classroom or outside of it. In-class use includes computer-based presentation, graphics, simulation, etc. Out-of-class use includes drill and practice, self-learning, problem-solving etc. Any combination of these could be used in distance education.

4. While experience with instructional computing has demonstrated the potential of computer technology in enhancing teaching, one should keep in mind that research on its effectiveness has not yet led to conclusive results.

5. An institution should not opt for computer use in teaching on the assumption that this might be a way of reducing the overall cost of instruction.

6. Given limited resources, prioritization is inevitable. When priorities for the computerization in a particular institution are established, consideration should be given to equity issues (e.g. appropriate balance for traditionally disadvantaged groups as well as among disciplines within the institution).

Recommendations

I. Planning of computer uses for teaching

1. To successfully implement the use of computers for teaching in a given institution, cooperation among individual faculty members, departments, institutions, corporations and governments should occur at the planning stage as well as on an ongoing basis. Overall planning and coordination of instructional computing activities are essential. The planning process should address the issue of establishing priorities for computing needs for teaching in the various disciplines. Decisions in this respect should reflect the specific objectives and priorities of each institution and be based upon recommendations from an advisory committee with faculty representatives from a variety of areas within the university. As well, user needs must be taken into consideration when priorities are established for computer use.

2. Given limited resources, an appropriate balance across the disciplines should be established with respect to the allocation of instructional computing hardware, software and support staff. Consideration should also be given to achieving an appropriate computer/student ratio.

II. Infrastructure

1. In the global decision-making process regarding support staff as well as acquisition of hardware and software, proper consideration should be given to the specific needs of instructional computing (e.g. adequate projection technology for in-class use of computers, computer labs specially designed for particular disciplines, etc.). While most of these needs may initially be met by a centralized computing centre, a gradual move towards distributed computing will facilitate instructional computing activities across the disciplines.

2. Provision must be made for regular maintenance of hardware and replacement of obsolete equipment used for teaching.

III. Curriculum decisions

1. Curricula for the various degree programmes involving teaching about computers should be updated regularly to reflect changes in the technology.

2. Students from all disciplines should be required to take at least one introductory computing class, offered centrally. The syllabus of such a class will also require regular revision as technology changes.

3. Whenever additional optional or required discipline-specific classes with a computing component are created, careful consideration should be given to integrating these classes into existing curricula.

4. Curricular planning should take advantage of existing technological support for multilingual computer applications.

IV. Faculty issues

1. Training of faculty is essential should an institution decide to implement instructional computing. Ideally, faculty training should go beyond the level of basic computer competence by familiarizing instructors with the various options of computer-assisted instruction from a discipline-specific perspective. Ongoing support to advise faculty with respect to instructional computing and to keep them informed about recent developments in the technology should be provided.

2. Faculty training should be offered to instructors across the disciplines to enable them to make well-informed decisions about instructional computing in their specific fields.

3. Equity concerns should be given appropriate consideration when planning and conducting faculty training programmes.

4. In faculty training programmes, it is advisable to focus on those packages which faculty may use both in their teaching and their research (e.g. presentation or data analysis software).

5. Because of the considerable amount of time and energy required for the development of instructional software and for its integration into existing class content, faculty achievements in this area should be appropriately rewarded.

6. Given limited resources, it is advisable to rely increasingly on faculty champions, both for formal faculty computer training and for informal support and advice.

V. Instructional software

1. All software used for teaching should be thoroughly evaluated before full implementation. Evaluation should be based on discipline-specific criteria.

2. Development of instructional software by academics requires careful planning in terms of resources (faculty and support staff time, equipment etc.) and software design. To develop high quality software, a team approach is recommended. In addition to a subject expert, this team should include a computer specialist as well as an individual who has expertise in instructional design. Institutions should recognize that research and development in instructional computing are interdisciplinary activities. Therefore, it is recommended that development projects and faculty workshops of an interdisciplinary nature be encouraged and supported by institutions.

3. To avoid duplication of efforts, cooperation in and coordination of research and development activities in instructional computing are essential. In order to facilitate coordination, evaluation and distribution, one or more institutions might be designated to function as a repository and clearinghouse for instructional software.

4. Use of instructional software, whether purchased or developed by academics, should be evaluated regularly by faculty as to its effectiveness in the teaching process. This assessment should take into account student feedback.

5. In countries where university courses are taught in several languages, consideration should be given to developing instructional software in each of these languages.

Computers in Research

The recommendations that follow are designed to provide an atmosphere in which academic research can gain maximum benefit from computerization. The recommendations are based on the following assumptions or definitions:

1. Research is taken to mean the broad spectrum of scholarly activity undertaken by academics in universities, including communication and the dissemination of information related to that activity;

2. Research is an important part of the mission of modern universities and, as a result, all academics are encouraged and expected to be involved in some form of research;

3. The use of computers can enhance research by making it easier to carry out a wide variety of activities and by permitting individuals to tackle problems whose solution would have been impossible before.

Recommendations

I. Infrastructure

1. In the very earliest stage of university computerization it is advisable to concentrate resources on a central computer facility that can be used for a variety of purposes and that can be centrally managed. As more resources become available and as more individual faculty members or academic units are able to obtain additional funds for computer purchases, micro- and minicomputers will become more widely distributed. Even then, a centralized infrastructure should be maintained to provide planning and advice as well as such services as maintenance of computing hardware and the network, responsibility for licence fees, major software purchases and upgrades, provision of support personnel and general training.

2. As more and more faculty purchase their own hardware and software, criteria should be developed to assist them. The number of different kinds of micro- or minicomputers, operating systems and general-use software packages (word processing, spreadsheets, databases, presentation graphics,

etc.) should be limited to allow for maximum compatibility, and to provide for effective maintenance and training. While individual faculty members or academic units may be free to make their own decisions, they must be made aware of the consequences of these decisions.

II. Effective Utilization For Research

1. Universities and granting agencies must recognize the importance of providing increased funding to pay for research computing. Every academic who wishes to make use of a computer in research should ultimately have access to one appropriate to his or her work. For most research problems the largest computers are rarely the most cost-effective. Microcomputers will be able to satisfy all but a small number of research needs. Very large mainframes or supercomputers should be provided only on a regional or national basis. Access to exceptionally large and powerful computer facilities can be accommodated through a network or travel grants.

2. Researchers are encouraged to seek external funds to support research computing but, even in the absence of funds, access to computing facilities should be provided.

3. To provide maximum access to E-mail, computerized library systems and large research or literature databases every desktop computer should ultimately be attached to a campus network which, in turn, should be connected to regional and national networks by reliable and high bandwidth media. Once a national network is provided for any purpose all other advantages automatically accrue.

4. Every effort should be made to develop cooperation between universities, government agencies and industry to fund research at universities and, as a result, to provide money for the purchase of computer hardware and software.

III. Training

1. Regular training in the use of hardware and commonly used software packages should be provided for staff who wish to make use of it. Readily available avenues of advice on appropriate hardware and software, help

with problems and frequent courses in the use of computing will go a long way to overcome academic inertia, phobias and frustration.

2. Training in generally used software, such as word processors, spreadsheets etc., should be provided by the central facility. Instruction in more discipline-specific software is best left to individual schools, faculties or departments.

3. It would be advantageous to recognize that, as part of their assigned duties, some faculty (product champions) could act as "facilitators" by being a resource from whom others, less knowledgeable in computing software and equipment, could obtain advice and informal training. If product champions are to be utilized there must be adequate recognition built into the university's academic reward procedures structure.

with problems and [illegible] courses in the use of computing [illegible] long way to overcome [illegible] for that purpose and [illegible].

2. [illegible] generally used software such as word processors, spreadsheets, etc., should be provided by the central facility. [illegible] discipline-specific software is best left to individual [illegible] departments.

3. It would be advantageous to examine [illegible] part of [illegible] some faculty [illegible] could act as "facilitators" by [illegible] a "course" [illegible] and equipment could [illegible] practical [illegible].

Administrative Computing

The recommendations appearing in this section focus on the use of computing in support of the university administration. Administrative computing is assuming an ever increasing role as the demands being placed on universities escalate, demands due to the increasing number of students, and greater demands for sound fiscal management and planning. As computing costs decline and methods change, universities must develop planning strategies to insure that the new technologies and procedures are employed effectively while, at the same time, meeting the fundamental goals of the institution.

Recommendations

I. Organization and Planning

1. When an administrative unit proposes a new system or a major modification to an existing system an advisory committee should be created, consisting of users from the administrative unit and representatives from affected academic and other administrative units. This committee should participate in the framing of system specifications which should be assessed to insure that they satisfy institutional needs and not just those of the administrative unit which is proposing the system.

2. Personnel from the computer centre should be integrated into the user departments and, when possible, should be given line responsibility in these departments to permit the expansion of career paths and to further cross training. There may also be advantages to integrating personnel from user departments into the computer centre.

3. The services of external computing agencies should be used to handle unusual or peak demands.

4. Universities should be encouraged to seek alliances with external organizations to promote the development of computing.

II. Systems

1. Out of the 11 categories identified in Volume III, *The Canadian Experience*, the three most important application areas in priority order are:
   - Student related Processing (e.g. examinations, student records)
   - Financial
   - Institutional Planning

2. Administrative systems should be integrated and run on hardware which does not use proprietary systems software. This will permit the development of an integrated network of on-line administrative applications which run on multi-vendor equipment.

3. Systems should perform as much of their task as close as possible to the user in order to capture the advantage of the cheaper computing available through a microcomputer on the user's desk.

4. Administrative software should be purchased. Alternatively, consortia, charged with the responsibility of developing or acquiring software, should be formed at the regional or national level.

5. Modifications of purchased software must be minimized to insure that updates from the vendor can be incorporated easily.

6. User departments should be encouraged to assume a greater role in the development of their systems ("end-user computing") but such users should be aided by consultants from the central facility. To guide users in the selection of hardware and software, the campus-wide computing organization should prepare a list of supported hardware and software products, and this list should be reviewed and updated at least annually. The creation of such a list will insure that there is compatibility with existing systems and that consultants have the background necessary to provide the user with needed advice. Users should be cautioned that if they choose an item which is not on the approved list they are assuming total responsibility for the product.

III. Infrastructure

1. When a computer system is installed it is essential that the infrastructure is adequate to operate it effectively. This includes space for the equipment, office space, work space, storage space, power, cooling, staff, maintenance and training.

2. Networks are required for the sharing of information and systems among users on the main campus as well as between the main campus and affiliated colleges or remote campuses. Ideally such networks should be electronic; however, alternate methods, such as floppy disk/tape exchanges, for the interchange of machine-readable data must be used when this is not possible.

IV. Training

1. The need for continual training is important and should not be limited to the immediate post-installation period or to one group. It should be provided to all individuals involved with administrative computing including computer centre personnel, administrators and general users from academic and non-academic units.

Technology Trends

The term **technology** is being used rather than the term **computers** because of the spectrum of technologies involved, from storage capacity to processor power to communications. One of the concerns often raised about technology and planning is that technology changes rapidly, making it difficult if not impossible to plan. Such concerns are rooted in attempts to develop plans based on a particular technology or a static view of current technologies. Planning should not be based on a specific technology but should recognize that there is continuous change in technology. When computing facilities could be found only in the computer centre, these changes appeared to occur at regular intervals as the centre upgraded its central facilities. As more of the general university community utilizes microcomputer and communications technology, changes appear to occur more rapidly. Indeed, changes in microcomputer hardware and software may reach the market more quickly and erratically than is the case with minicomputer and mainframe upgrades. However, the most significant technological change that has occurred is that individual members of the university community can aspire to have their own microcomputer or small computing facility. Thus, the user community is becoming more aware of issues like hardware obsolescence, software upgrades and incompatibilities between hardware and software.

The growing use of microcomputers by individuals and departments across the university represents the most significant change in the form of computing since the introduction of computers. The successful management of technology over the next decade will be measured by effective management of this change. As decision-makers face this challenge they must understand that competent management of change brought about by technology involves the able management of people. Although the pressures may seem greater owing to the rapid pace of technological change and the increased involvement of the university community, decision-makers can take comfort and strength in and plan from the knowledge that the parameters of the management problem are familiar.

Recommendations

I. Computing Power

1. The institutional computing plan must be based on the massive increase in computing power and storage capacity that will become available in this decade. Likewise, this plan must move towards implementation of networking within the institution with connection to regional and national networks.

2. The computer centre must work closely with all sectors of the institution in order to apply these improvements in computing and communication capacity to pending and unsatisfied administrative, research and teaching needs.

3. Taking advantage of the declining cost of computing hardware, senior management must shift priority from the purchase of computing capacity to building the necessary infrastructure to support the effective use of the increased computing resources. The available capacity and the user demand for access to this capacity will cause infrastructure costs, such as training, networking and maintenance to far outstrip the computing centre's financial ability to purchase the resources needed to provide these services.

II. Technology Trends and Management Issues

1. The computer centre must prepare for the necessary changes in its management style, from the management of computing facilities to the management of people. The emphasis needs to shift from controlling resources to providing services as users increasingly require infrastructure support rather than access to centralized processing power.

2. Management of central computing facilities and provision of services to users involve issues of power and control. The computing centre traditionally has controlled and allocated a scarce and unique resource of critical importance to the user community. As it acquires more powerful microcomputers and becomes more knowledgeable about computing, the user community will move away from the influence and control of the central organization. Tensions and conflicts may result. Problems should be viewed by senior management as a sign of growth and a transition

towards maturity within the institution. Management must not attempt to mandate rules governing the dynamically changing relationships between the computer centre and its users. Rather, the computing centre must be helped by being provided with additional resources to strengthen its role as a service department.

III. Services

1. The computer centre must facilitate the use of technology to invigorate the teaching, research and administrative sectors of the institution. Fulfilling this responsibility will require that the computing centre understand the role of all sectors of the institution and seek out an active part in advising these sectors in how to adopt new technologies. At times, it will be appropriate for the computer centre to work closely with units in incorporating technology. That is, the computer centre should not limit its activities to technology that is to be generally available to the institution.

2. The computer centre must advise senior management about the location and sharing of facilities to be housed outside the computer centre. In all such cases, the computer centre should be the agency responsible for infrastructure support. This may eventually result in computer centre support staff working in user areas across the institution.

3. The computer centre must effectively communicate the actual costs of computing, including maintenance, operating and support costs, to senior management and to the user community. This will facilitate the making of informed and optimum decisions about the acquisition, allocation and usage of computing.

4. The support of networking and large database activities is clearly a centralized function which is best handled by the computing centre.

5. The computer centre should identify and pool resources to update and acquire new technology to be housed in the central facility and make it available to the general university community. For example, the computer centre might work with several research project groups to combine individual small project computing budgets in order to purchase a shared computer.

6. Infrastructural support will be required from the computer centre by all sectors. It will not be possible to make computer centre staff familiar with every piece of software and hardware being used in teaching and research.

However, the centralized staff will be able to utilize their experience to aid teachers and researchers in attempting to solve problems.

7. Support from the computer centre should take the form of training and on-going consulting. Consideration should be given to training the computer centre consultants so that they are able to deal with both hardware and software problems.

8. The consulting service must be readily accessible to users. Large concentrations of users will be best served by computing centre staff located in close proximity to them.

9. Maintenance is an issue for all sectors and is undervalued by many until a problem occurs. Maintenance can be approached in many ways and solutions must fit the local context. However, it should be handled through the central computing facility. Maintenance contracts are usually the most expensive option but are necessary in many cases. For example, when parts are not available from the vendor and used equipment cannot be purchased in order to salvage parts, then a maintenance contract is the only viable approach. Self-maintenance may be an alternative.

10. The computer centre must develop strategies to utilize old technology when innovations such as the purchase of used equipment or self-maintenance will permit the equipment to be maintained in an affordable manner. These strategies may include the movement of equipment between units, including the computing centre.

11. Maintenance is a service that, along with other infrastructural services, raises questions of a charging policy that must be decided by senior university decision-makers.

IV. Computer Centre Needs

1. The institution must provide for the training of its computer managers and staff in the management of technology, realizing that effective management of technology requires communication skills and the ability to work with the user community. Training must not be limited simply to technical material about new technologies.

2. Sufficient budget allocation must be provided so that the computer centre can carry out its expanding role.

Summary and Conclusions

I. Policy and Planning

The implementation of a decision to computerize a university rests on an understanding of a complex web of internal and external factors, including:

1. Availability of financial and computer-related resources (hardware, software, technical support staff);

2. Opinions and attitudes of the decision-makers regarding the perceived role and likely impact of computers on the educational system and the society at large.

An understanding of these factors becomes part of the policies formulated by those agencies concerned with education - the ministries of education of the federal and the state governments, national organizations charged with the responsibility of allocating financial resources to and coordination of the universities and institutions of higher education (e.g. the University Grants Commission in India), and national and international foundations. In India, for example, the *National Policy on Education 1986* observed that "as computers have become important and ubiquitous tools, a minimal exposure to computers and a training in their use will form part of professional education" and envisaged the use of computers in several aspects of college and university education and management.

While such a policy at the national level does indicate desired societal goals, the planning and executive agencies at the national, state and university levels will need to make feasible plans to realize these goals. A policy represents a general course of action or intent; a plan is a more specific and detailed indication of the actions envisaged to be taken during the specified time-span. It is a course of action based on a consideration of the availability of relevant resources and their allocation corresponding to the prioritization of the objectives set out in the policy. The task of resource allocation is not simply one of cost benefit analysis in the economic sense, but one of finding the most effective way to build the computer network whose building blocks are people, technology, money and space. In view of rapidly changing computer technology and expanding needs, universities need to formulate an adequate policy to do the following:

1. To generate finance for the capital investment necessary for hardware and software purchase and updating;

2. To strengthen centralized as well as distributed computer facilities;

3. To provide adequate computer facilities to those faculty members who may not have external funding for their instructional and research needs.

This also requires formulation of an appropriate system of levying charges for different user groups in consideration of their likely impact on academic activities. Due care must be taken to ascertain that, while the objective of the charging system is to achieve an appropriate utilization of the available computer facilities, avoid waste, and generate revenue for recurring expense, the policy should not result in unequal computer access for academics from different departments or for students from various socioeconomic backgrounds.

The process of computerizing a university or an entire system of higher education involves changes in both technology and human relations. Careful planning is required because there are many misconceptions, and misunderstandings, as well as unrealistic expectations, as to what computers can do. There is no simple formula or one "right way" to go about computerization. The planners must weave together various technical components with people's needs and interests. Sometimes, the absence of a relevant policy at a higher level leaves a lot of room for the planners to use their judgement. Similarly, the policy and programmes of other sub-systems can have a considerable bearing upon the means the educational planners can use to realize the goal of computerization. For example, the policy of the government in levying import duties on foreign computer hardware and software can have an affect on the goal of computerization in the educational sector.

Educational planners need to take into account the available and rapidly changing computer technology, the nature and extent of computer competence of entering students, the role of private agencies outside the educational sector in providing computer training on a commercial basis, the immediate and more long term needs of the various industrial, commercial and other organizations for trained computer personnel, and the attitudes and values of the players in the educational sector who will have to be torch-bearers for implementing any plan for application of computers in the teaching, research and administrative functions. There is a dynamic relationship between policy formulation, planning and the plan's execution. As the broad policy framework is the guiding force for planning, the execution of the plan suggests those areas of the policy that might need review and modification.

II. Organization of Computing

In writing the early drafts of this volume, the phrases central computing organization and computing services department were often used instead of computer centre. The problem was to describe the unit or department that would be responsible for computing generally across the university. **Central computing organization** seemed to allow for centralized responsibility while recognizing the growth in distributed computing and expected increase of computing facilities located around the university. **Computing services** stressed the importance of service to the university community. However, the term **computer centre** is the most traditional choice and, perhaps, best reflects the typical organizational structure at a university that is in the early stages of implementing distributed computing and expanding its service offerings.

The recommendations in this volume and the case studies found in the other two volumes clearly envisage a wide range of activities and responsibilities for the computer centre. The computer centre should be responsible for central facilities, computing personnel, support for distributed facilities such as networks, maintenance services and consulting services. The infrastructural support that the computer centre must be capable of providing to the university community is limited by the centre's budget. Budget allocations to most computer centres are based on the model of a central computing facility with centralized staff. Funding for maintenance, training and consulting support for both the centre itself and the user community is inadequate at best. The need for increased funding support for the computer centre is critical.

There are numerous ways in which funding levels could be increased. The university could internally reallocate resources to provide increased resources to the computing centre. In order to emphasize the service requirements in computing, some universities have reallocated resources to the user community, allowing the users to decide on the services to be purchased from the computer centre. The university could encourage its members to more actively seek external research and development funding for computer facilities. Business and industry are the primary beneficiaries of computer literate university graduates and could be approached to cooperate with universities in establishing better computer facilities. The computer centre and academic departments might be able to sell training or access to computing facilities to business and industry. Differential tuition or service fees could be considered for those disciplines that place heavy demands on the computer centre.

A contentious issue at many universities is the use of a charging policy for computing facilities and services. The computer centre could charge for maintenance service, for computer time, for disk storage, for printing or for many other services and resources it provides. A charging policy certainly stresses to the user community that computing is a scarce resource to be utilized wisely. However, any policy that charges for resources also restricts access to those resources and will be viewed from that perspective by many in the university community. Charging extra tuition or usage fees in disciplines requiring extensive computer use could limit access by disadvantaged socioeconomic groups. Researchers with insufficient computing funds or teachers in disciplines just beginning to use computing will perceive that the computer centre charges too much for computing and they may not use computing to the extent they should. The important fact that the computer centre lacks the resources to satisfy the computing needs of the university and to help the university to fulfil its role in society will be missed. A charging policy should always be discussed as only one component of the more general issue of appropriate levels of funding support for computing, particularly early in the process when the demand will far exceed the available resources. Because of the impact on all areas of the university, such discussions and the resulting policies belong in the domain of the **senior decision-makers** at the university.

All instructional, research and administrative computing should be the responsibility of a computer centre which is directed by a member of the university's senior management, an individual with a rank equivalent to a vice-president. This individual must hold this rank in order to effectively advise other senior management on the selection of technology and provision of services for and among administrative, research and teaching applications.

The nature of a university implies freedom of choice, and the scope for individual academics to make decisions that would not be possible in an industrial or business setting. Microcomputers, for example, will be easier for an individual or department to purchase as technology costs continue to decrease. The recommendations of this volume should not be interpreted as suggesting that decisions relating to the purchase of personal microcomputers can only be made with the approval of the computer centre. This would imply budgetary restrictions that are probably impractical or unacceptable at any university. However, the computer centre will be offering services for a limited range of hardware and software. Occasions when an academic or administrative unit decides to purchase outside the advice, support and services of the computer centre must be allowed in a university setting. Increased numbers of such decisions should motivate the computer centre and senior managers to review the range of services offered. The result may be an expanded list of supported hardware and software. However, it is important that all computing users recognize that the computer centre cannot be called upon to support hardware or software that the centre has neither approved nor recommended.

There should be a strategic plan for computing which is reviewed and updated yearly. There should be a policy advisory committee composed of senior academics and administrators to advise the computer centre regarding policy and budget matters, and revisions to the strategic plan. There should also be a mechanism to elicit input and recommendations from the user community about operational problems and needs. A user committee composed of both academic and non-academic users of computing, especially the product champions, should meet regularly with staff from the computer centre. The chair of this user committee should be a member of the policy advisory committee so that the user community has a means to make recommendations to the policy makers.

One of the major services offered by the computer centre to the university community should be training. The computer centre should offer short courses that match the services it provides. For example, it should offer training in the use of the microcomputer packages it supports or the data analysis or database software used on the central facility. The focus of this training should be to get novice computer users favourably and comfortably started in their use of computing. Continuing consulting services would then facilitate the users' movement into more complex applications or techniques. The computer centre should cooperate closely with academic units which can provide expertise in this training. Academic units may teach classes that contain similar material to the computer centre's training programs and vice-versa, and they may offer non-credit training that requires discipline-specific content best taught by an academic in that discipline. Cooperation and wise use of knowledgeable individuals should determine the best approaches to teaching and training.

Equity must be a paramount concern guiding all decisions about computing as computing is a tool that can be judiciously applied to improve the situation of traditionally disadvantaged groups within society.

III. Training

The recommendations given earlier are concerned with the computerization of the various functions within a university: teaching, research and administration. The importance of training has been emphasized for each of these functions. The essence of the recommendations with respect to training may be summarized as follows.

In order to successfully implement new technologies, a learning process among users must take place. This process not only includes learning about the technology (i.e. acquisition of new skills), it also takes into account user attitudes like resistance to or fear of technology.

Training does not only include formal instruction but also informal help and advice from product champions and other individuals with computer competence. The main responsibility for formal training lies with the computer centre. In addition to initial training, provision must be made for training on an ongoing basis.

Whenever training programmes are organized, equity issues, such as an appropriate balance between genders or among disciplines, should be taken into consideration.

Two target groups can be identified with respect to computer training in universities: academic staff and non-academic support staff.

Training for academics has several components: familiarization with the computer technology, introduction to instructional computing in various [illegible] software [illegible] specific training [illegible] be achieved at the [illegible] level training [illegible] instruction and [illegible]

Training [illegible] computer users [illegible] technology-related training and should be offered by the computer centre on an ongoing basis. [illegible] should [illegible] training of computer centre staff in communication and interpersonal relations skills [illegible] interaction with the user [illegible] management of technology.

Given limited resources, the role of product champions [illegible] informal training and [illegible] cannot be overemphasized. To encourage [illegible] there should be [illegible]

[illegible]